A 1000 X BETTER

A 1000 X BETTER

A Rebel by Design · The Work and Vision of Kirsten Blazek

RIZZOLI
NEW YORK

New York · Paris · London · Milan

"If you want a golden rule that will fit everything, this is it: Have nothing in your houses that you do not know to be useful or believe to be beautiful."

· WILLIAM MORRIS ·

First published in the United States of America in 2024 by
Rizzoli International Publications, Inc.
300 Park Avenue South
New York, NY 10010
www.rizzoliusa.com

Book Design: Thunderwing

Publisher: Charles Miers
Editor: Ellen Nidy
Production Manager: Rebecca Ambrose
Managing Editor: Lynn Scrabis

Printed and bound in China

2024 2025 2026 2027 2028 / 10 9 8 7 6 5 4 3 2 1

ISBN: 978-0-8478-9960-9

Library of Congress Control Number: 2023683424

Visit us online:
Facebook.com / RizzoliNewYork
instagram.com/rizzolibooks
twitter.com/Rizzoli_Books
pinterest.com/rizzolibooks
youtube.com/user/RizzoliNY
issuu.com/rizzoli

FOREWORD BY EMILY HENDERSON

IT'S NOT VERY OFTEN that you meet a fellow designer whose aesthetic can boldly transcend you into another world and keep you wanting more. That's how I felt when I first came across Kirsten Blazek. She has a wow factor that stops you in your tracks. Although I had been following her career and seeing her projects on Instagram, we actually met in person when I was pulling product for a photo shoot from her warehouse in Pasadena. We instantaneously clicked and bonded over our mutual love of bohemian style and vintage treasures. That afternoon, I walked out of her warehouse with chic furnishings for my shoot, a newfound appreciation for the American Southwest, and a lifelong friend.

As fellow design moms and business owners, we both face the daily challenging task of balancing a growing design business while also raising young children. Wallpaper samples and algebra homework rarely go hand in hand, and it takes a lot of mental fortitude to find a harmonious equilibrium between being a working mother in a creative, unpredictable industry. You have to be tough, resilient, fearless, and rebellious in your approach to everyday life.

What is a rebel? To me, a rebel challenges the notions of tradition and following the crowd. A rebel is someone who questions authority and values individual expression. A rebel stays true to themselves and does not conform to what society expects of them. Kirsten is a rebel in every sense of the word, and that is what makes her stand out as a designer and a friend. From her nontraditional approach to design, unpredictable and courageous design choices, and, most notably, her nontraditional path as an interior designer, Kirsten is always up for a challenge and never takes the easy way out.

As a former ICU nurse for many years, Kirsten's entrance into the world of design was anything but typical. She started her career in design after discovering her passion for interiors

while staging a house on the market for a friend. That house ended up selling for well over asking because of Kirsten's creative staging and reimagining of the house, which clearly made a huge impact. It takes guts, determination, and perseverance to quit your nine-to-five job to pursue your lifelong passion and follow your dream—and that's just what Kirsten did. Now, she is one of the biggest names in the design industry, with a cult-following on Instagram and a wide roster of celebrity clients.

Kirsten's viewpoint on design is unlike any other, and you never know what to expect with her projects. Her expert design style is full of charm and personality; her interiors are functional, practical, and authentic. Her boldness and passion for design continues to inspire me, and her eclectic and soulful style will always keep you guessing and compel you to dive deeper and look beyond the surface.

For readers of my website, Style by Emily Henderson, Kirsten's work is a never-ending source of inspiration. They love discovering her gorgeous projects and learning more about her backstory. She has a masterful way of reimagining and transforming any space. Whether it's a ranch style-bungalow or a modern, ground-up construction, Kirsten magically captures the essence of a house and makes each space look a thousand times better than before. Her first book, *A 1000 X Better: A Rebel by Design*, will give you the unique opportunity to peek inside her world, to discover her unwavering journey, and to immerse yourself in the endless beauty of design and nature we all crave. I am deeply honored to be a part of her book and to be connected to her inspiring journey.

opposite · A carefully curated collection of meaningful objects is an amazing way to make a home feel layered and personal. If you respond to an object's call, buy it—it will become something more than a decorative object.

above · This room was decorated for my daughter, who was ten years old at the time. I wanted to play with the native California plantings outside her room, so I went bold with this cactus wallpaper. It also incorporated all the colors that were used throughout the house.

opposite · We were blessed on this project to work with creative clients, one of whom had created the amazing ceramics in their collection. This job is still one of my favorites to date and felt like an innately symbiotic collaboration between client and designer.

THE
INTRODUCTION

THIS IS NOT GOING TO BE your typical design book nor am I the typical designer story. When I say I am a rebel by design, I'm not referring to that 1950s greaser blazing down the road on a Harley Davidson with a cigarette hanging out of his mouth. I'm the rebel who was brave enough at almost 40 years old to listen to what the universe was saying to me and to push past the fear that said "you're too old and this is crazy." If there is anything you take away from my story or work, I hope it is that anything is truly possible when you walk the road less-traveled to see where it goes.

First, a little time spent on where I began, so to better understand where I ended up. I was born and raised in Edinburgh, Scotland, by two parents who were loving hard-working. In those days most people had a very "don't stray too far outside the box" approach to living. The arts or a career in an artistic field was not something that was celebrated or encouraged. The Scottish are very salt-of-the-earth people who are wonderful in many ways, but during my days there this always came from a very practical point of view. So I grew up feeling like a square peg being forced into a round hole, and that caused me to rebel in the ways that were available to me. I turned vegetarian after becoming obsessed with Morrissey and dyed my hair pure white. I was constantly changing around my room or finding some interesting hippie piece to hang from the ceiling. I was always stuffing that little artist down deep, yet letting it out in other ways that I felt I could get away with. I know I must have driven my parents crazy at times, but I was figuring it out as best I could.

In those days, when you chose a major in college it had to be something that would pay decently after university. I always found people fascinating and by nature loved helping anyone, so I decided to become a nurse. Interior design probably wasn't even on the menu back then, and I wasn't even remotely ready to accept my true nature yet anyway. I completed nursing school and made my parents happy about my path forward. Though there was always a feeling of yearning for

something more, I actually enjoyed being a nurse in the early adult years. It taught me to really listen to people and gave me a sense of pride helping them heal, which I didn't know at the time was bringing me closer to being an artist. The little firecracker in me came out on weekends with my friends, when I would dress wild and go see bands or dance all night at a club. Everything seemed planned out at the time: I could grow older as a nurse in Scotland, meet a safe man, and have a few kids. Well nothing could be further from the truth. The whispers of the feeling that there was something more for me out there never went away.

One night when I was 24 years old and out at an Irish bar in Edinburgh with some friends the direction of my life changed forever. I met a charismatic young American man who I immediately fancied. We had an inseparable romantic affair for the month he was there. It was exhilarating being with someone from a foreign land I had never been to and learning about a culture I had only read about. I felt drawn to him in a way that was new to me. When he finally left I was properly hooked and couldn't wait to talk to him or see him again. I didn't realize it at the time, but part of this was my inner burning to find out about the world and more about who I was. We talked on the phone all the time, and for the first time I decided to hop a plane and go to America to visit. It was that first visit to the US—I would visit three more times after that—where I realized how connected I was to living there, and having a new adventure. I wanted a life in a different country, and so when he asked me to move to the States with him I agreed without hesitation. My parents and friends thought I was out of my mind, maybe I was, but I have always had a brave and fearless side.

So there I was living in San Diego, California, working as an ICU nurse, and spending my days with my American partner. I eventually made friends, married that man, and we soon bought a house together. It was this house where I first started to find a little of my design acumen, and though it was quite infantile compared to where I am now, I found something that I enjoyed outside what would only be described as a nice quiet San Diego life. We eventually decided to have children, which was quite a challenging process. If anyone has ever gone the IVF route, then you know exactly what I am talking about. We ended up having two wonderful kids who to this day teach me so much, and it was worth all the trouble in the world to do so. Once again I figured this would be my nice typical life, only this time in San Diego and not Scotland. However, my husband getting transferred for work to Los Angeles would dramatically change the course of this story for good.

We moved to Altadena, California, where we bought this amazing storybook house from the 1920s that was in need of some love. I had by this time left nursing to take care of the children full time and was in need of something to feed my ever yearning artistic heart. I decided I would make the rehabbing and decorating of our home my project. I thought deeply over every detail, went all over vintage furniture shopping, and cut a lot of hours on my new project. The house spoke to me, and it felt like it wanted me to help it become what wanted to be. So I listened, I worked, and for the first time acted as a designer in some ways. Still it's not like I was truly aware this is what was happening. I was a firmly entrenched being a wife and mother of two, and at this point had no idea this would later become my career. Over several years I finished the house completely, and as I did so my marriage was unraveling. The little things come to show you what's next sometimes, so that what is about to end can turn to the new. This house was my path to the new me.

He and I tried to make it work as best we could, but eventually it was quitting time and the divorce happened. I stayed in the house and he moved out, but now I needed a way to provide for my single life. I needed to provide for my kids. I started looking and applying for nursing jobs again, but something in me just didn't want to do it again. I didn't know what I could do, but I just knew it wasn't supposed to be that. Then one day a mother from school came over to my house to have some wine. She walked in and was floored by what she saw, and asked who did the design work. I told her that I had done all of it myself. She then said words that would change things for me for good: "You should do this for a living. I have a friend who is looking for a designer for her house in Malibu. I am going to introduce you to her." I was both exhilarated and petrified by the idea, but I somehow just *knew* it would be OK. I pushed past my fear and drove out to meet her friend shortly thereafter.

I ended up doing that first job for next to no money, and it was very challenging mostly because I didn't know what the hell I was doing just yet. However, I did know that I had a natural gift for the work and trusted that I would be able to pull off the job to the client's liking. Wow, my mind was spinning, and I knew this is what I wanted to do. After that, I certainly couldn't ever go back to nursing, but I needed to actually make money doing this work. The universe works in mysterious ways when you start moving toward something, and it certainly did in this case.

I went to meet with my real estate agent friend Jen to talk about possibly selling real estate. I obviously still hadn't fully accepted that what I wanted to really do was even possible. We sat and talked for a bit, and she said that she hadn't asked me there to talk about real estate. She had seen my house and heard about the job in Malibu, and she asked me had I ever thought about staging houses. I honestly didn't know that was a thing, but if it was a way for me to keep feeding my newfound passion for design then I would surely start thinking about it now. She had a Frank Loyd Wright house that hadn't had an offer on it in six months, and she was looking for someone to properly stage it to help it sell. I didn't need to hear much else—I was all the way in.

Jen took me to the house, and when I walked in I had the feeling that I would have every time since—a feeling that the space was talking to me. It was telling me

above · I am pictured here with my brother. Our travels around Scotland with our parents were an important part of my childhood—not only were we creating memories, but I later realized I was passively absorbing nature, culture, and a sense of ancient history.

opposite · The energy of these old lands run through me like a mystic ley line core and is both grounding and humbling.

· 14 ·

"My parents and friends thought I was out of
my mind, maybe I was, but I have always had
a brave and fearless side."

"...and I reached out for it with everything I had."

what it wanted to look like. I knew I had to make this house look as if someone was actually living in it. But without any real furniture to do my work, I had to borrow things from Jen and her partner and anywhere I could get my hands on what I needed to make it come all the way to life. While putting this space together I had that feeling one has when they first fall in love: it was purely exhilarating and revealed to me that I had a real gift for this work. But it was also a ton of work as I was doing the whole install myself with the help of one mover. When we were done it looked fantastic, and that was quickly confirmed when six days later the house sold for more than asking. I guess I was starting my own staging company, and I was going to call it A 1000 X BETTER!

I didn't realize it at the time, but I had created a niche in the market that really didn't exist yet. Staging homes with the eye of a designer and making them look truly lived in was something unique at the time. I began getting requests from everywhere to stage houses, and I started my business with just me and that mover from my first job. As my financial resources grew I started to build my library of furniture, paintings, dishes, plates, glasses, and decorative pieces. I would rent a U-Haul and drive around to vintage shops looking for unique pieces that I could use. It was such an important part of helping to build my aesthetic and personal taste. For me it was a design school education by doing. There was also a good amount of manual labor, hauling furniture and pieces in and out of the house—so it certainly wasn't the most glamorous school.

Four years later I had five employees and two warehouses full of materials. We were crazy busy, and any normal person would have been satisfied to keep things going the way they were. However, I knew I had more to offer the world as a full-fledged interior designer. I waited for the right opportunity to present itself, which turned out to be my own house, one that I bought in Linda Vista. You will hear and see more about later, but I will say now doing a full interior design on my own home once again changed my life

for the better. My home was published in pretty much every design publication you can think of, and I started getting interior design requests. It was time to take my career to the next level, and the years of staging houses and running my business had not only prepared me for this next step, but it had also given me the confidence that I was ready.

Many years later, after becoming fully established in the design world through numerous projects, A 1000 X BETTER no longer does staging jobs. We have now grown to ten employees. Fearlessly following my instinct so many years ago has lead me to build something that I am proud of. I never thought I would be here yet always knew I belonged here. I wear the fact that I am self taught with gratitude and pride, because I learned everything I know by doing, making mistakes, failing, getting back up, and asking for more.

This has been quite a journey I have been on, and through it all I have learned so much about who I am. I have a level of self-acceptance and confidence in that human in the mirror now. I have tattoos because I love them. I will rock a Valentino dress with snake-design cowboy boots because it makes me feel right. The more I create the more I become, and the more I become the better I get at creating. My work is my passion and the gratitude I feel for it, and the wonderful loved ones I have in my life, is infinite. It doesn't matter that it happened later in life or that I'm not classically trained, what matters is that it happened at all.

It is with the utmost appreciation and gratitude that I offer my work and words in this book for you to hopefully enjoy. I have tried to give you something a little different by letting you deeper into my mind as a designer while showing you the work I have created so far. This career and life of mine was something that was presented to me as a possibility, and I reached out for it with everything I had. Some things are just meant to be. They are by design. Thanks for taking the time.

opposite · The color of autumn leaves always takes my breath away—for the perfect yellow, look no further than a tree in transition. Another example of a flawless yellow is found in this ocher-colored building, Culross Palace, which stands in the Scottish royal burgh of the same name.

ONE

EVERY JOURNEY
HAS A FIRST STEP

> "Twenty years from now you will be more disappointed by the things you didn't do than by the ones you did."
>
> — MARK TWAIN

CHAPTER ONE

NOW THAT YOU KNOW where I came from and the life I left behind, let's have a chat about that massive step I took to become who I am today. I bought this Pasadena house at a baby stage of my design journey, and I decided was going to put every ounce of me into it. I didn't have a real thought-out plan, something that I would absolutely never do again nor recommend anyone do ever… not ever. However, I am a doer, and when something scares me I lean into it instead of running away. With my staging business well underway and trust in my eye growing, it was time for me to translate that experience into a full interior design redo. What better place to start with than with my own newly purchased home, one that was badly in need of some love and care.

There is nothing that can turn you into a knowledgable master of your craft more than doing the thing yourself all the way. For a self-taught designer this project was both the most rewarding and most challenging one I have ever had. Imagine if you had a car laid out in pieces in your backyard and had to put it back together. You would tear your hair out, make tons of mistakes, and take longer than an experienced mechanic would. Then, before you know it, that car is back together and sitting in your driveway. You would never ever do that again, but now you under-stand how every little inch of that car works. This was my car in a million pieces, and by the time I reached the point of the

photos you see I knew I was a real full-blown interior designer who would never stop sharing my purpose with those I am fortunate enough to create with.

I wish I could show you what this house looked like before I ever stepped foot inside it for the first time. No one wanted to go near it with a ten-foot pole, but the house spoke to me loudly. When I say this house needed absolutely everything, I mean it was a pull-the-detonator, ignite-the-dynamite situation. There is not a single thing in these photos that didn't have to be redone. I could feel it, I could see it in my mind, and all of it came rushing to me with an otherworldly clarity.

When I say every journey has a first step I'm not talking about the first house I staged. Sure that was a great feeling and an initial proof of a path, but it was this complete redo that showed me for the first time who I am. This home is who I am. It is the birth of my purpose and the fruition of my gift that I share now on any project I take on. It doesn't matter whether or not you get struck with purpose and have a moment like I had that day. What matters is that you get moving toward the goal. I strive to give all my clients that same feeling of "we really did something here, didn't we?" For me, there is simply no better feeling in the world.

opposite · This room in my previous house was a tricky shape—long and narrow, with an offset fireplace and all the windows at the end of the room—that made it difficult to place furniture in a balanced way. To solve this, I created separate areas within the room that all had their own purpose. An interesting wallpaper helped the room feel more cohesive while keeping a neutrality that made it easy to add decorative objects. The painting above the fireplace was a family heirloom of my then-partner and was the inspiration for the color palette.

The backyard of this house had been completely abandoned when we moved in and needed a refresh. I worked with a local gardener and changed all the plantings to California natives and succulents. As with any backyard, I wanted it to be a continuum of the house aesthetically.

This room was originally cut off from the kitchen by cabinets on one side of the fireplace and a bar on the other. I removed all of that and opened up the kitchen, creating two distinct spaces—a dining area and a seating area in front of the fireplace that was warm and inviting. The fireplace's original brick was painted a dark brown-black to ground the space.

"The privilege of a lifetime is to become who you truly are."

· CARL JUNG ·

I am most attracted to a muted and nature-based color palette. Both of these photos are a reflection of how subtle colors can have a large impact: The photo above was taken at sunset in Ojai, one my favorite places. The fireplace shown opposite was a styling job that required minimal decoration because the shape of the fireplace itself was so attractive.

TWO

FIND YOUR
UNIQUE

> "You've got to try it. You've only got one trip, you have to remember that."
>
> — IRIS APFEL

CHAPTER TWO

I THINK CONSTANTLY LOOKING AT yourself and finding new things about who you are is one of the great joys in life. I know today I am so different than I was five years ago, or ten years ago, or maybe even three hours ago. It's our own personal evolution and the more we reach for discovery the closer we get to finding out who we are. Everything I have been through in my life to this point has made me a better artist, a better mother, a better partner, a better dresser, and a stronger purveyor of what makes me unique. I don't question my taste as much as I used to when I was less sure of who I was. That's the beautiful thing about aging—for every wrinkle earned you find another few pieces of the puzzle that is you. As a designer, I live for getting in tune with my clients and helping them curate a space that is truly unique. To create a space that is both honorable to the home, and specific to those who reside in it is everything.

Every client, every home, every moment, and every challenge is the most wonderful opportunity to build something unique that embraces you in a way nothing else can. Your home is you, and when I tap into you I can see it coming together in my mind. I have always thought the job of a good designer is to act as a visual guide for people looking to create an environment that doesn't clash with themselves. Having a strong sense of my own taste and style allows me to help someone find theirs, and this is the balance of collaborating. I check my ego at the door, but I never check my opinions or sense of self. Without those, I would simply not be any help to anyone.

For me, sometimes the smallest of things can spark a whole design. It can be a pattern on a pillow, a vintage rug, or a reclaimed tile that helps me see how a room wants to look. It is the simple things that can lead to the biggest dreams of what a space is and wants to become. I spend quite a bit of time getting to know the people I design for, because the more I have a sense of them as people the better I am at guiding them through the process. Having a real sense of each unique person allows me to mix and match and play with the palette until it looks just right.

I encourage you to think about things you like. Ask yourself why you like them. This process can refine your taste and thus help you form a strong sense of what it is you want to achieve with your home. Any successful relationship depends on clarity of communication. This work is a collaboration, and when someone knows they're unique then the process can yield something pretty unforgettable. Design is such a personal thing and, for me, when it's done right it is for you and you alone.

opposite · The layout of this Pasadena home was originally a series of small and dark rooms. The clients were a young, creative couple who wanted a sense of light and space, so we opened up the divisions between the dining room and kitchen and used a light paint palette to make it more visually cohesive. Ultimately, this made the rooms feel much larger and more inviting.

193/900

This bedroom was part of a large remodel we did on a house that had been flipped badly. We raised the ceilings, added an open light fixture with an interesting vertical shape, and dressed the windows with curtains to create warmth in what was now a larger, more open room.

opposite · This small kitchen was part of an ADU (Accessory Dwelling Unit) conversion—a space within a house converted to a separate residential dwelling—completed for use by an elderly parent. Maximizing while maintaining the overall aesthetic, a completely open space was of the utmost importance. We maintained a neutral color palette of black and white and used simple shapes that aligned with the house's midcentury style.

below · This bathroom in another midcentury house was designed for a bachelor client who wanted a combination of drama and simplicity. We stuck to simple with a black-and-white palette and brought the drama with this beautiful panda marble slab for the backsplash.

this page · This kitchen was done in a midcentury modern casita that we remodeled for use by an elderly parent. We wanted to keep it clean, but functional, since every inch mattered in this small space. Along with all of the practical items needed in a kitchen, we incorporated some bar seating and a bookshelf. We raised the ceiling to add height and bring the eye up; French doors brought in more light and provided easy access to the backyard. The new doors, in addition to a bright and fresh color palette, took the room from dark and divided to light and breezy. We were also able to fit an island, which could be used for entertaining as well as meal prep.

opposite · We opened up the dining room to the kitchen and kept the color palette similar so that it felt like a true extension.

this page · Sometimes the simplest things can kindle a desire to create something unique. This beautiful old building in Ojai did just that for me. The stone's layering and colors translated into the perfect palette for a kitchen with a Spanish character that we had been hired to remodel.

opposite · Our task here was to create a non-traditional kitchen that still felt like it belonged in a Spanish home that had midcentury inspirations. We layered a soft color palette and warm wood tones to effect a mix that was both modern and rustic.

"I am going to make everything around me beautiful—that will be my life."

· ELSIE DE WOLFE ·

this page and opposite · This was a dilapidated garage that we converted to a diminutive ADU (Accessory Dwelling Unit) with a kitchen, bathroom, and living areas. The structure needed to maintain the same standard of living and aesthetic of the main house. For the interior, we layered items like wallpaper and a wood-clad ceiling to achieve a finished and cohesive look. For the exterior, we wanted a dark palette without using flat stucco walls, so we added board-and-batten.

this page and opposite · A complete remodel of this house included a thoughtful kitchen redesign. The client wanted a modern space but one that still felt warm and inviting, so I blended a combination of natural materials like tile and wood cabinets with more modern, clean lighting and plumbing fixtures. The large and bright bedroom needed a touch of warmth and color, so I chose textiles and objects that made it feel cozy and lived-in.

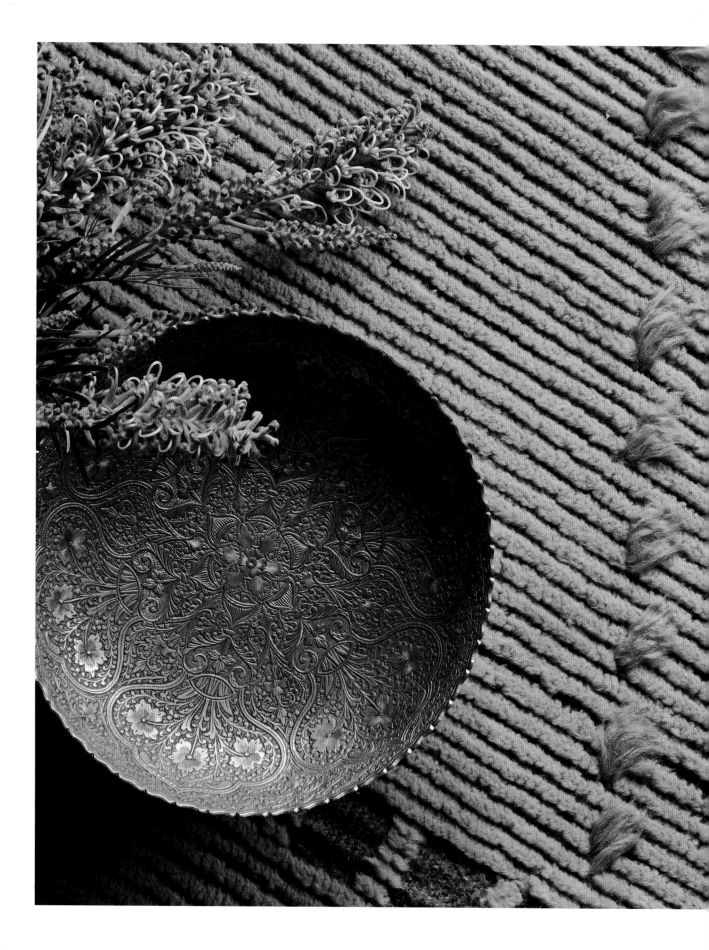

THREE

LET'S TALK
LAYERING

> "The right amount of complexity is what creates the optimal simplicity."
>
> — DAVID ALLEN

CHAPTER THREE

I ABSOLUTELY LOVE walking through the seemingly never-ending booths of the Rose Bowl flea market on a hot Pasadena summer day. For me, it's like being the captain of a ship navigating rough seas in search of lost treasure. I am looking with laser focus for the few gems amidst the many stones that will help complete the transformation of the space I have been entrusted with. A beautiful handmade pot, a vibrant kilim rug, a handwoven basket, a vintage lamp in need of a dusting, and that painting hidden at the end of a rack—these are the treasures that help a well-planned, well-furnished design truly become three dimensional. It is what layering is all about.

Layering is everything; without it all you have is a flat space that feels lost. It's that perfect light fixture over a kitchen countertop that dances with the spirals in the wallpaper set against the linen undulating drapes. I love a fancy custom handmade sofa as much as anyone, and moving a wall out of the way to open up a room makes my heart flutter. But the precise intention of layering the space is what really sparks my Scottish blood. It's the subtle mix of color, texture, and pattern with just the right amount of decorative pieces that evokes the feeling of a room. Too much and you're in the clutter jungle, too little and for some reason that room will always make you feel lonely like a Sunday morning matinee. I have spent so many hours

walking the layer tightrope to get what you see in the finished product to its beautifully potent potential.

Creating something that is three-dimensional is always the goal with my work. I want the client to walk into their new space and feel it coming out to greet them. I think you have probably noticed by now that I absolutely love splashing wallpaper in my designs. Wallpaper creates a sense of drama and depth in a room, when it's used properly, and is really the start of the layering process. There is always a wall or two in any project of mine that says, "have a little fun with me." I am always happy to oblige! From there I can start playing with light fixtures, displaying art in unusual places, and putting vintage finds in the right spots. I take the foundations of my designs and keep dabbing that canvas until it is just right. My paint palette contains elements seen and unseen that help you feel and experience the space. My hope is that as you look through the photos in this chapter your eye will delve further, thus revealing each room's depth and true intention. As an interior artist my work is never fully finished until those layers pop out and say hi.

opposite · Layering a space starts with many things, but one of our favorite ways is using vintage rugs and textiles to bring in color and a sense of levity, history, and craftsmanship. This combination features some favorite rugs that I had picked up from thrift stores and flea markets.

this page · Layering can come into play in many ways, and a well-styled shelf can add a lot to an overall design. On this kitchen shelf we mixed vintage items with newer ones, all in a similar color palette, to create an authentic moment.

opposite · While the hard materials in this bathroom lean more modern, adding a vintage rug, a softly shaped stool, and Turkish towels take it from spare to warm and layered.

"Innovation is often the ability to reach into the past and bring back what is good, what is beautiful, what is useful, what is lasting."

· SISTER PARISH ·

this page · Layering is a way to provide dimension. For example, without the draping plant, this brick wall would feel flat and lifeless instead of alive and vibrant. The same rules apply when decorating a house, and plants are the perfect way to breathe life into a room and add depth.

opposite · I am not risk adverse to a bold wallpaper choice; in fact, a well-chosen wallpaper is one of my favorite ways to take a room to a whole new level of feeling. Wallpaper not only adds visual interest but is the ultimate way to add a base layer to an interior.

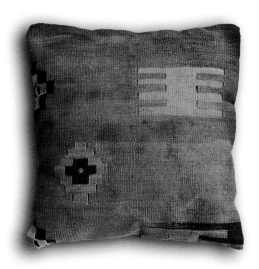

this page · Our mandate here was to add some furnishings and decorative layers to this already beautifully remodeled Tudor-style house. The bold wallpaper was the ideal way to give the dining room some extra personality.

opposite · We added layering to this modern bathroom in a Japandi-inspired new construction by elevating the tub on a deck and adding a shelf along the back wall. A vintage oil painting helps tamp down the newness of the room.

this page · This building I saw in Rome was a perfect example of how artistry can also extend to the exterior of a building. The fresco-style painting here makes a statement but also blends in perfectly with the other buildings around it.

opposite · This bathroom was originally a series of three small rooms that we opened up to create one large space. It didn't have a lot of natural light, so we selected a pale-colored tile to enhance the feeling of brightness.

Be discerning with your layering. This tailored-back room in a modern home is paired with a small collection of decorative objects to help it breathe. This gorgeous console with an interesting repeating pattern brings plenty of interest on its own. You always want to pay attention to minimize anything that might compete in room and so that all the pieces play together in a synchronized way.

Living with Wood

FOUR

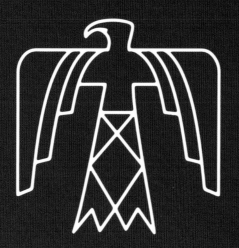

COLOR IS
EVERYTHING

> "Color! What a deep and mysterious language, the language of dreams."
>
> — PAUL GAUGUIN

CHAPTER FOUR

YOU KNOW THAT FEELING you get when someone walks into a room with a fabulous green dress, and then you slowly scan down and see they paired it with the most beautiful strappy tan heels? I will certainly turn and stare at a combination like that, and that is how color works its magic to evoke a visceral response. Color can be dramatic or playful or whimsical or subtle, but whichever emotion you choose for your colors to speak, they have to work as a unit. This is why every home and every room I design has to have a color palette that makes you feel the whole house as one.

I love mixing colors in a house so that they speak to one another and have a nuanced relationship with each other and a through line as you experience the space. As a Scotswoman with the soul of an old cowboy, my attachment to earth tones is quite strong. My primary color choices almost always start from the earth, and I carefully inject them throughout without being too overt about it. The perfect mix of colors is the ideal way for me to achieve balance in a house, which is a fine line because if a color is off even slightly then everything is thrown off throughout. A particular shade of blue may be beautiful, but ask yourself what it looks like when the sun hits it in the morning?

Color should be the first thing that greets you when you walk in the front door and should continue to whisper in your ear as you walk through the rest of the house. This is the art of using color with intention in a house. Once I've chosen my main color palette I can then play with little splashes of other colors around a space. In the right hands color can make a house unforgettable.

While there are really no wrong colors (well, maybe a *few* come to mind), there are certainly wrong places to use them and wrong partners to mix them with. I like to build the dimension of color in a room by using textiles, art, objects, and decor. Color, like layering, is supposed to create depth in a room. I view black and white as working neutrals—a palette that is easy to add to—and almost always use them to ground the space.

Color around your house should also be taken into consideration. For any design to feel right it has to be symbiotic with the environment—both inside and out—that it inhabits.

As you look at the rooms in this chapter, look for the color foundation in every room. Everything has a purpose color-wise and like a band of talented musicians have to play together for it to work as a whole conceptually. In my line of work, color is everything.

opposite · Color is all around us—it's in everything we see, so always keep your eyes open and pay attention. To understand color, start in nature. Mother Nature rarely puts bad color combinations together, and this beautiful flower is the perfect example of tones that work in harmony.

Went Out to these Lakes. And From
  she Took a Handful of the Star Water,
ght these Back to the People. And she
  Handful to Each Person and Hung it
  s Neck, like a Medallion. These
  s of Star Water Glowed like the Stars,
  One of the People could See by them
  ery Other One was. The People Lived
  Until One Man Became Angry and
  Star Water Into the Fire. He then Went
  nder the Ground, in an Earth Lodge,
  the Other People
  o the Fire, and so Went to Live in
  ges Under the Ground. Only the Girl
  with her Star Water. She Remained
  Grow in a Beautifully Painted Lodge.
  iful Young Girl Took the Fire that
  the Pieces of Star Water and Took
  to the Lakes. She Took Back the Star
  t had been Thrown Into the Fire and
  Each Piece to its Lake. She had One
  aining, and at this Lake she Made

  Elk Came to her at that Place and the
  to her, if you Hang the Star Water
  y Neck I will Keep it for you. I will Give
  you when you Need it."
  ve it to the Elk and she Returned to
  People were. She Remained in her
  odge, and she Lived in this Great Lodge.
  of the People Continued to Live in their
  ges. One Day the Elk Came to Visit her
  d the Elk and Ate with him. The Elk
  returned again. The Fourth Time he
  he Spoke, saying, "You will be my Wife
  r Husband, and we will Live Together."
  and they Hung the Star Water Outside
  Lodge.
  hers of the People were Naked. They did
  how to Live Together, and they had

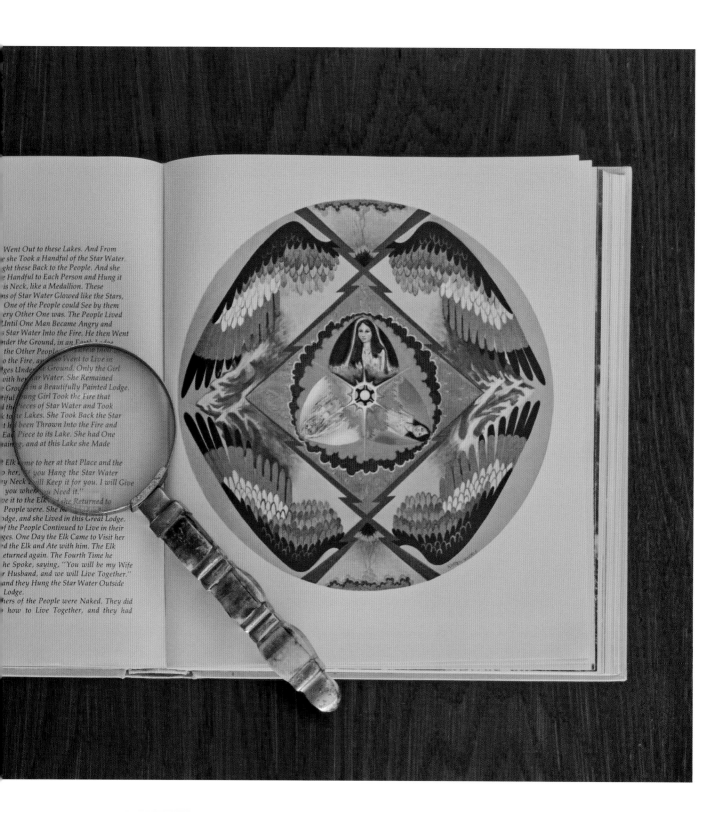

this page · This seating area was built as a cozy nook at the end of a long, spacious bathroom. The one thing that kept the whole room feeling cohesive was a unifying color palette. The client's vintage painting from her childhood found a home here, supplying not only color but a touch of personality.

opposite · One of the first things I decide on when I start designing a space is a color palette. For this bathroom, this wallpaper I fell in love with became the building block for the rest of the principal suite.

"As a Scotswoman with the soul of an
old cowboy, my attachment to earth tones
is quite strong."

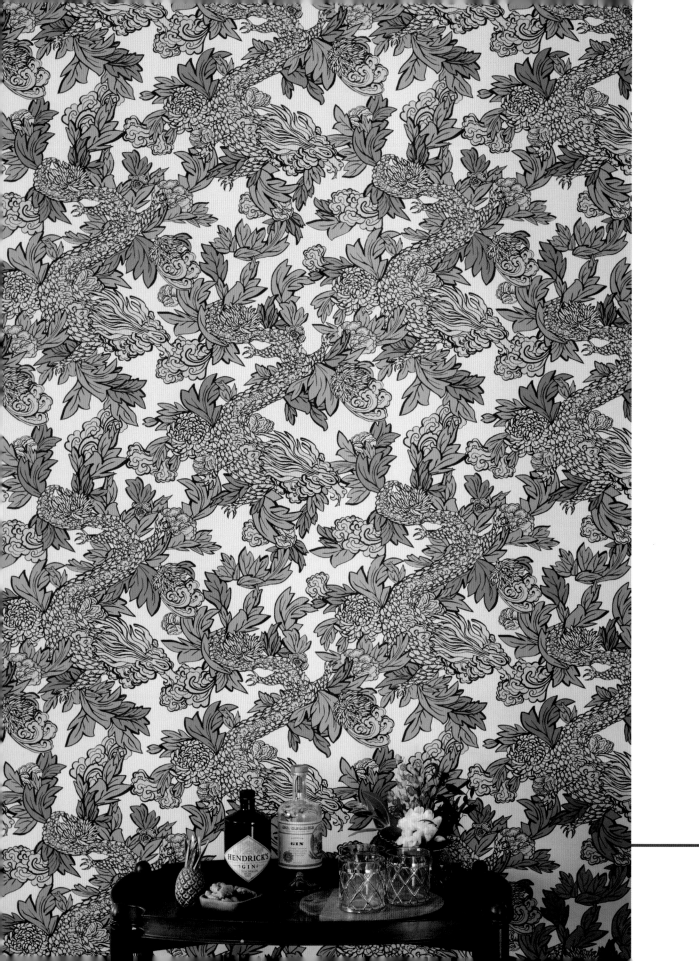

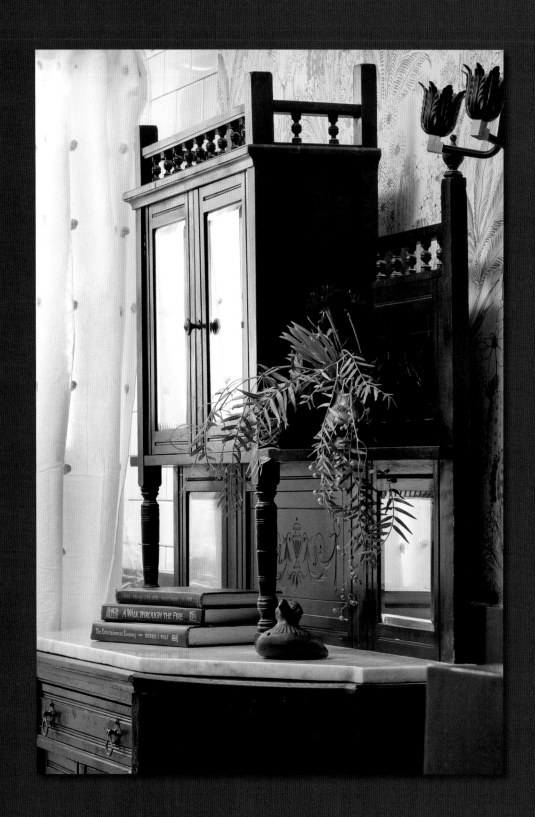

"Color is a power which directly influences the soul."

· WASSILY KANDINSKY ·

Prothero

FIVE

A
REFLECTION
OF YOU

> "The best rooms have something to say about the people who live in them."
>
> — DAVID HICKS

CHAPTER FIVE

ONE OF THE ABSOLUTE best parts of my work is that I get to collaborate with people. Buying a house is a brave choice to begin with, and then to trust in me to bring it to a level they couldn't imagine is a great responsibility. Most of us want nothing more in life than to be seen and heard. A home is a very tangible part of fulfilling that desire. The home in the photos in this chapter is the very definition of this.

I was lucky enough to work with friends of mine who had purchased a beautiful Spanish-style house that was in desperate need of some reimagining. They are a creative couple with a highly elevated sense of taste. Their natural design sensibility leaned toward midcentury, which meant we had to find a way to marry that with the house's traditional architecture.

I love figuring it out and helping a house become a part of my clients' dreams. For the kitchen in this house, we collectively decided to use a balanced approach for the cabinets—warm rustic wood with a flat-front surface—a nod to Spanish-style and midcentury in one look. The backsplash tile had a classic midcentury pattern, but the muted creams and grays softened the look so as not to clash with the house's more overall look. We ended up threading the needle between both styles and creating a beautiful eclectic vision. What started as a challenge ended up becoming a marriage of styles that worked perfectly for everyone.

Your house should be a part of you and about you. It's not just what it says to visitors, but how it makes you feel when no one else is around. My work allows me to build relationships with lots of different people from different backgrounds with unique tastes and personalities. When I have the honor of designing a space for someone I do everything I can to make the space feel and sound like them. Their house should be the place they can't wait to return to. If this happens, then I know my work is done. Home is where you go when you need a warm embrace and to see yourself in its surroundings.

opposite · The client who owned this house was an artist who makes incredible ceramics, and it was important to her that we incorporated a sense of handmade organic materials into her design. We took that into consideration for this bathroom, with the custom concrete sink, plaster walls, and natural wood elements like the mirror frame.

Open shelving was an important part of this kitchen design—all of the dishware and serving items had been lovingly made by the client. We selected wood tones for the cabinetry and shelving that harmonized nicely with the colors in her ceramics and made the shelving styling look cohesive.

honoring the light and magic of our creative community

"Only the truth of who you are, if realized, will set you free."

· ECKHART TOLLE ·

this page · For these first-time homeowners it was so important that we made their house feel like them, despite the fact that for the majority of the remodel they were out the country. They had to trust that we were listening and interpreting their sense of style. This kitchen felt very tired but the cabinets themselves were handcrafted and had lovely lines, so instead of replacing them we refinished everything and had additional matching cabinets custom-made where they were needed. A tile backsplash, new lighting, and the window trim painted a contrasting color add even more interest.

opposite · Despite the fact that this house was supposed to be sold after we remodeled it, I still added interesting items to make it feel personal, even though conventional wisdom is that houses for sale should feel impersonal. Placing some unique items around—like the vintage oil painting under the window—gives a house personality and that personality is often what makes people connect with a property they're looking to purchase.

this page · The intriguing bold geometry and simple color palette of an old vintage rug I owned provided inspiration for the striking bathroom (opposite). It was designed very much with the client in mind, a sophisticated bachelor who wanted it not only to feel authentic but also to fit seamlessly into his midcentury modern house.

SIX

EVERY HOME
WANTS TO BE HEARD

CHAPTER SIX

THERE IS NOTHING that makes my insides scream more than walking into a cheaply done flip job for sale, where all the soul and character of a house is torn out only to be replaced with hollow nothingness. A house is an organic entity that holds the echoes of the hands that crafted it and those that once walked its halls. Yes, a home needs an update over time, but its character and its history is something I never step on. I listen to what a house wants and then embrace that fully. Breathing new life into a house with history is like giving a wilted plant the water it was desperately hoping for on a scorching hot day. When you walk into a house you're thinking about buying and there is that "this is the one moment," that's the house's character and history speaking to you. When a house calls to you, it means you are listening to what it is saying to you and you're meant to be there.

The house featured here is to this day one of my absolute favorite projects. The clients, who were away working in a different country, purchased this house sight unseen. They then uttered the words that every designer dreams of hearing but so rarely does: "We trust you and want you to do whatever you want with it. We like what you like."

The house was situated in a beautiful part of Malibu Canyon, surrounded by greenery with a creek running behind it. At one time the house had most certainly been a ranch house on a vast farm. However, the current owner had turned it into a frenzied design from my worst nightmares. There were reds, yellows, and greens on the walls and mismatched wood paneling everywhere. It was an absolute mess, but thankfully the original amazing character was still intact, which was whispering to me telling me what it needed and wanted to be. It had these beautifully crafted midcentury cabinets, which we kept and completely refurbished to their original glory. There was also an incredibly unique wood barn door, original to the house, that was the gateway to the living

room. It was these elements that spoke to me and became the baseline for the completed design that you see in the photos. Maybe somebody else would have gutted this home or simply torn it down and built something else. However, I saw something special that needed me to bring it back to life for the clients who put their absolute trust in me. I owed it to them, and I owed it to the house that had barely survived its previous owner. To achieve that for two clients I came to know and love is still one of my favorite times spent with a design. I can't adequately express how important it is to have that real trust between designer and client. The most successful design projects always happen when a client trusts the designer to fully realize their vision. When this happens, it is almost always better than anyone could have imagined.

A house sometimes feels like it finds you instead of you finding it, and when you listen to what is emanating from it, then you can truly continue the story it tells instead of wiping it away forever. Character is the lifeblood of a house, and to bring it back to life is the most fulfilling part of my work.

opposite · When we visited this house for the first time I immediately fell in love with its potential. It was an old ranch house in a Malibu Canyon with good bones, but it unfortunately had been torn into a million styles and was begging to be reunited with itself. This window nook area we created was originally a useless empty space, and I saw the perfect opportunity to make it both beautiful and functional.

"Most people these days chase new things, new houses, new cars, new objects. But they don't realize that old homes, old cars, and old objects have something that new things don't have— their history and culture."

— AVIJEET DAS

this page and opposite · The doors in this bedroom opened up to a backyard with an ancient and massive California oak, a creek running behind the property. and horses on an adjacent property that you could hear when the doors were open. We wanted to create a space that infused all this outside atmosphere into the bedroom—a tranquil space where the clients could feel at one with the natural world without even going outside.

The hallway leading to the bedroom had been painted an oppressive yellow, so we changed it to a bright white to make the passageway an inviting way to access the bedrooms on that side of the house. Luckily, the original ceiling lights were perfect and we didn't need to replace them.

this page · Vintage art adds layers and depth to a simple monochromatic vignette. A quiet bedroom moment designed for reading.

opposite · This living room had mismatched wood everywhere, so we had to carefully decide which wood to leave and which to leave original. Here, we decided to unify the whole room by painting the stone fireplace and wood wainscoting the same color, but we left the beautiful original mantel and wood trim. When modernizing a space, I like to always leave original whatever still makes sense in the overall redesign.

this page · We transformed this room that was open to the dining room and hallway into an intimate and cozy moment where the family could enjoy time together and sit in front of the large fireplace.

opposite · This office from a whole-house remodel we did was a space begging for new life. It had been painted a dark color that made it feel very traditional, so we left the original fireplace but painted it a warm white and added modern lighting and furniture to breathe a sense of vitality into it.

"Be faithful to your own taste, because nothing you really like is ever out of style."

· BILLY BALDWIN ·

SEVEN

DETAILS ARE THE EYES OF DESIGN

CHAPTER SEVEN

THERE IS SIMPLY NOTHING that bonds and shapes and forms a whole picture more than the details. The eye gazes upon something and responds to it in a macro way, but it is the little details dancing together that matter. You wouldn't be wowed by a beautiful dress without the perfect shoes, earrings, rings, nails, and hair adorning the person wearing it. When you look at these pictures of my work, and hopefully have a positive emotional response, that's the room glowing through its own intricate details. In my line of work there are no accidents or last-minute random add-ons to a house or a room. Everything you see was meticulously thought out and planned before it was ever incorporated into the design.

Getting into what I'm talking about a little further: We did the design on a midcentury post-and-beam home (some photos of it are in this chapter) that was extremely outdated and had a nonfunctional floor plan that needed to be re-imagined. We had to literally rip it down to the studs and start over. Details are what tie a home together, and this house's impressive vertical lines became the most important detail to be used throughout. The same vertical lines are echoed in the wood cabinets, the millwork at the top of the stairs, the staircase banisters, and the bathroom vanities. That's the through line that makes the house visually interesting. We also took flagstones and carried through with them from the front driveway into the entirety of the first floor. Details aren't always color or the little things, sometimes they can be lines and the use of space that help the eye see its beauty for the first time. Every little thing has to be planned and thought out, and that devil in the details is what makes or breaks that plan.

Sometimes the details in design can help to heal a person when they walk into a finished work for the first time. Another of my favorite projects was the second house in this chapter for that very reason. My client had just lost his

husband and decided that updating his midcentury house would help him work through his grief. I believe our houses are living, breathing entities that take on the energy of their owner, so the solemnity of this job hit me right in the heart. The details for this job were deep, rich, sexy colors and bold lines that were in keeping with his taste. The graphic panda marble splashing all the way to the shower is an example of this. Through these details we were able to flavor his space and give it a feeling of something fresh ahead for him. Design can heal and the details can provide comforting companionship.

My art is sometimes the painstaking obsession over every inch of every detail that goes into creating a successful and pleasing design. My imagination runs wild sometimes, but it is always grounded in a plan. There isn't too much in this life that does not require attention to detail, and that is most certainly the case for me. When it feels right, it looks right, and when it looks and feels right, the details are doing their magic.

"The details, that's what the world is made of."

— WES ANDERSON

this page · The principal bath suite in this house had a large closet area that you had to walk through in order to enter the actual bathroom, and it was important that it felt like an integrated element. A completely customized closet system was designed not just to be functional but also to amplify the overall design.

opposite · This new staircase, to the right of the front door, was essential to setting the tone for the whole house. The vertical wood posts carried from the ground to second floor, and the slats were left open to create an airiness. The design sets the stage for the strong sense of architectural elements as you move through the house.

opposite · This round table with an interesting base shape sits as a nice juxtaposition to the strength of the vertical lines behind it, and it is a good example of how to mix both soft and hard shapes when designing your home.

this page · We took most of this house down to the studs, but the wood ceiling was original and still in good shape, so we chose to refinish rather than replace it. The wood ceiling adds warmth and depth to a large room otherwise devoid of character.

"Nature is the inspiration for all ornamentation."

· FRANK LLOYD WRIGHT ·

this page · In this large, wide upper hallway we needed to add interest to a wall that would have otherwise been just plain painted drywall, so we decided to build a custom cabinet that added some storage but that also provided dimension and space to display decorative items. The cabinetry was also a clever way to hide an unsightly electrical panel.

opposite · This ensuite bathroom was part of a guest bedroom that was likely to become a child's bedroom. We went with a soft color palette but kept the design elements—vertical cabinetry and stacked tile— consistent with the rest of the house.

this page · This deeply colored brick wall served
as a jumping off point for designing the bathroom
shown opposite. We wanted to recreate the feeling
this simple wall was giving us—linear and moody
but warm and inviting at the same time.

opposite · When choosing tiles, I often naturally
gravitate toward a field tile and the simplicity they
lend to practical areas like showers. In a bathroom I
generally prefer to add details and interest in the
millwork, hardware, and lighting. If wallpaper makes
sense, then I advocate for that as well. I prefer to
keep the base simple and work in the details with
less permanent elements.

This kitchen was part of an ADU (Accessory Dwelling Unit) in a new build, but the intention was to carry the same level of finish to the accessory dwelling. The kitchen was designed in a way to complement the one in the main house but not replicate it exactly. We wanted cohesiveness, but the new design elements we introduced make it feel unique.

EIGHT

A HEART IS THE
LIFEBLOOD OF ART

"Art is my life and my life is art."

— YOKO ONO

CHAPTER EIGHT

I AM AT MY VERY CORE AN ARTIST, and I look at the entirety of my experience in this life through that lens as much as possible. There are so many things in my life that inspire me, and when I am being present and allow it to happen, my work gets deeper and better as a result. I found my purpose a little later in life, and I have no hesitation in making every moment of this chapter of my life has to offer me. Whatever your artistic field is, if you're not out there feeling all of it then you are doing a disservice to your gift. For me, the execution of any design requires a heightened intuition of all the senses. It has a touch, a sound, a soul that speaks, and a spirit that opens the eyes. These are some the things that inspire me to tap into my art a little better.

I love music and going to live shows and watching my favorite artists perform. What an incredible gift to be able to take an instrument and make sounds come out of it in unison with others, resulting in people dancing and singing along with joy. Orville Peck is probably my great adult music crush. I love his beautiful voice, thoughtful lyrics, stage presence, and uniquely fabulous choice in how he presents himself through fashion to his audience. Being bold and being you is something that always makes me gravitate toward someone. Music feeds my artistic soul, and I need that to be satiated in order to use it in my own work.

I also love to travel as much as possible. Traveling is an explosive massage to my senses, and I try and soak up even the tiniest of details along the way. There is nothing more inspiring than walking into a perfectly curated hotel that grabs you from the eyes to the heart. Beautiful textiles in the lobby or that vintage brass tub overlooking a French veranda. I feel the places I go as much as possible and engage with my environment and those who inhabit it. I always travel with an underlying intention of learning about myself and growing the bounds of my creativity. I bring back a little part of my adventures with me to help further polish and define my work. Travel is when imagination meets reality, and I have never missed a chance to get out there and find it. Design is about building a specific world for someone to inhabit, and what better to expand that possibility than packing a bag and going out into the great big world where we all reside.

Along with more of my designs, the other photos in this chapter speak to the artist that lives inside me. Although it's not typical to share this side of things in a design book, I wanted you to get a sense of how other sources of inspiration find their way into my work. At the beginning of this book, I explained that I'm not your typical designer, and I wear that with pride—from my obsession with fashion, music, cowboys, colors, or the tiniest of things that most people wouldn't notice —and I think that is reflected in my work. These photos are the parts of who I am, and the things that inspire to keep finding more of who I am.

opposite · In order to create, I need to travel, and when I do have the chance to get out of town I keep my eyes open—you never know when you are going to see something that could inspire you in the future. This tiled wall in Ojai is a beautiful example of something you could easily walk by without paying attention to, but when you do become aware of your surroundings, the rewards can be enormous.

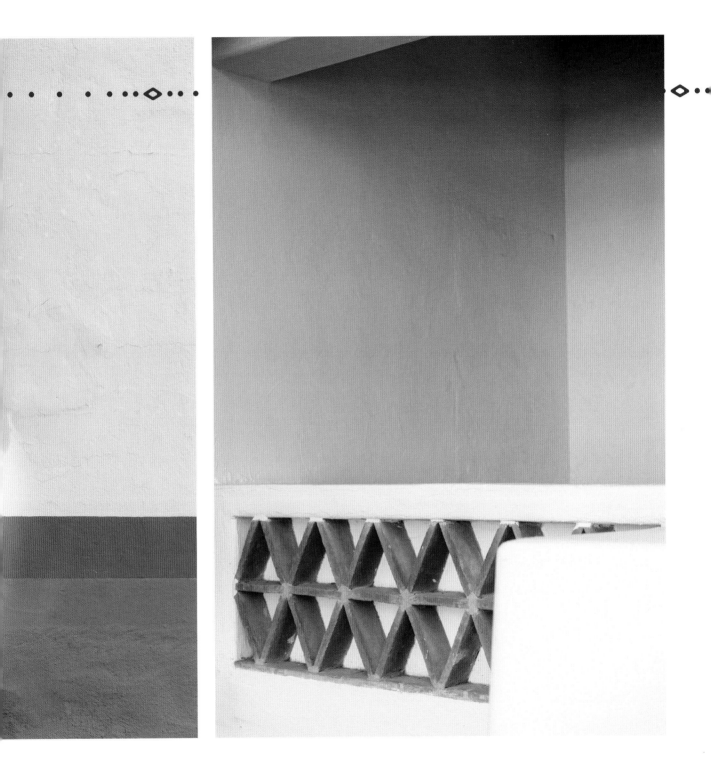

this page · This wall in Los Angeles has a certain beauty despite being somewhat in disrepair. Visiting local art galleries is one of my favorite ways to find inspiration.

opposite · A built-in desk that was detailed with wood to make it feel warm but unassuming.

ART GALLERY

"Have no fear of perfection. You'll never reach it."

· SALVADOR DALÍ ·

this page · This custom bar was detailed out to complement the living room and kitchen—evidence that even practical areas in your home can be beautiful.

opposite · Small, simple moments can have as much impact as bigger ones.

this page · I loved this tile but didn't want to create a niche in the shower and possibly introduce another material, so I mounted this simple brass wall soap dispenser instead. It was functional and fit in seamlessly.

opposite · This bathroom we created for our own studio space in a historical building was thoughtfully designed not only to play with all the colors we used throughout but also to complement the building as a whole. I lovingly styled it with items collected throughout the years, so it also feels very personal.

"Always keep your eyes open. Keep watching. Because whatever you see can inspire you."

· GRACE CODDINGTON ·

This kitchen in a Craftsman-style spec house from the 2000s wasn't in sync with the actual style of the house. We redesigned it to have authentic Craftsman shapes and details but infused it with a modern take that complemented the young family that owned it. We used mixed materials to create a sense of elegance and make the large kitchen feel more unique and unexpected.

this page · A play of light and shadow inspired by my travels and a mix of materials all work well together—a good lesson in how the simplest vignettes can help form your design eye.

opposite · My love of the Californian desert landscape sometimes bleeds into my work, and this cactus wallpaper is a reflection of how the places you visit can indirectly influence your creative choices and leave a lasting impression on the spaces you create for yourself.

This exterior patio porch from my old house was one of our favorite places to relax, and it felt like a true reflection of the way I designed the interior spaces of that house—relaxed, layered, and filled with personal items of significance to me.

CREDITS

All photography in the book is by
Alex Zarour of **Virtually Here Studios,**
except the photographs on the
following pages, which were shot by
Michael P. H. Clifford: pages 2, 18, 31, 48,
49, 102, 103, 126, 164, 205, 214, 215, 233,
and the front cover image

This book is set in various weights of
the typefaces Apris and SCTO Grotesk,
both developed and designed by type
foundry **Schick Toikka** (Berlin/Helsinki)

ACKNOWLEDGMENTS

Only when the stars align can something as magnificent as a book happen.

But the true stars in my life are the people who have been there for me every step of the way.

To my dedicated team, both past and present, I want to express my deepest gratitude for your invaluable contributions to me and A 1000 X BETTER since the beginning of this incredible journey. Without each and every one of you, none of this would have been possible. It takes a village to bring good design to life, and you are an integral part of it all. I want to extend a special thank you to Courtney Holshouser for being the solid foundation behind it all.

To Alex Zarour and Michael P.H. Clifford, the talented photographers featured in this book, I cannot express my thanks enough. Great design is nothing without equally great talent behind the lens, and your remarkable work brings our vision to life.

To Jake Demaray, who was able to take my feelings and thoughts about design and skillfully transformed them into the words you see written in the chapters of this book. I am eternally grateful to you and could not have done this without you.

To all my friends who uplift me, challenge me, and help me grow into a better, more creative and refined person—I hold deep love for each of you. Thank you for sharing in all of life's experiences with me. I want to acknowledge my sisters, Traci Fleming, Tamara Honey, Jennifer Parker Stanton, and Rachael McIntyre, each of who have played unique roles in shaping who I am.

To my family, who may have questioned my choices at times but nonetheless loved me unconditionally. And to my children, who have witnessed my hard work without ever complaining, you humble me and inspire me to be better every single day. Never stop being true to yourselves.

To our clients, I am incredibly grateful for your trust, support, and friendship. Being a part of your lives brings me immense joy, and seeing you fall in love with the homes we've created together is the ultimate reward.

To all the vendors and collaborators we work with, I want to express my sincere appreciation for your talents and skills. Each one of you has played a crucial role in making our projects come to life.

To Monica Conti and Sonia Rodrigues from Rodrigues PR, thank you for your unwavering support of AXB. We couldn't have achieved any of this without you.

To Thunderwing, your genius is truly remarkable, and it has been an absolute pleasure to witness your transformative work on this book that turned it into something truly beautiful.

To all the women out there wondering if they can pursue their dreams, I want to say: you can. You can do anything.

And finally, a heartfelt thank you to the Rizzoli team for making all of this possible.

Kirsten Blazek
Los Angeles · 2023